What makes you smile?

Do you smile when you put on a hat?

Smiling

Gwenyth Swain

For my mother, Margaret Coman Swain,
most likely the first person to make me smile

To find out more about the pictures in this book, turn to page 22.
To find out more about sharing this book with children, turn to page 24.

The photographs in this book are reproduced through the courtesy of: Jeff Greenberg, front cover, pp. 12, 15, 17; © John Elk, back cover, pp. 8, 13; Voscar, The Maine Photographer, p. 1; © Patsy Tissembaum, p. 4; Australian Tourist Commission, p. 5; Brian A. Vikander, p. 6; © Jean S. Buldain, p. 7; Ruthi Soudack, p. 9; Ken Kragen, USA for Africa, p. 10; © Stephen Graham Photography, p. 11; ELCA photo library. Used by permission of Augsburg Fortress, p. 14; World Bank Photo, p. 16; Piotr Kostrzewski/Cross Cultural Adventures, p. 18; Russell L. Ciochon, p. 19; © Luke Golobitsh, p. 20; Jay Cossey/Images, p. 21. The publisher has made every effort to contact the copyright holders of the images enclosed within this publication. Please call or write if you were not contacted.

Copyright © 1999 by Carolrhoda Books, Inc.

First published in the United States by Carolrhoda Books, Inc.,
c/o The Lerner Publishing Group 241 First Avenue North, Minneapolis, MN 55401 U.S.A.

First published in Great Britain in 2000 by Zero To Ten Limited
46 Chalvey Road East, Slough, Berkshire SL1 2LR

A CIP catalogue record for this book is available from the British Library.

ISBN 1-84089-179-3

Manufactured in the United States of America

Do you smile for the camera, just like that?

People smile when they think about
the ones they love.

Sometimes we smile ...   just because.

Being with friends is a good reason
to put on a happy face.

So is being with your family,
all in one place.

Do you smile when it's a beautiful day?

Do you smile when it's time to play?

Smiling is a way of saying, "I'm happy!"
without words.

It's a way to let your feelings be heard.

Nobody smiles all the time,
and that's just fine.

Sometimes we're sad or mad.

Sometimes we're shy.

Sometimes we can't even say why.

But when that sad time ends,
put a smile on your lips.

Smile big.

Smile often.

Smile just like this!

More about the Pictures

Front cover: A smiling child waits outside a food store in Vilnius, the capital of Lithuania.

Back cover: In Indonesia, a boy sits on top of a water buffalo.

Page 1: On Grand Manan Island, off the east coast of Canada, a girl shares a smile.

Page 3: A boy sits on the sands of Guyana, a country on the northern coast of South America.

Page 4: In Mexico City, Mexico, a girl has fun wearing a sombrero, a hat with a large brim.

Page 5: These two Aboriginal boys live in Australia. The Aborigines were the earliest known people to live in Australia.

Page 6: A girl in Rajasthan, India, looks up with a smile.

Page 7: Friends in India give a Hindu greeting called *namaste*.

Page 8: A group of boys in Mali, a country in West Africa, hang out together.

Page 9: A family gathers outside a house in the Guangdong Province of China.

Page 10: A young woman smiles at a cool breeze in the deserts of Sudan in northern Africa.

Page 11: Three girls play peekaboo in Omaha, Nebraska, USA.

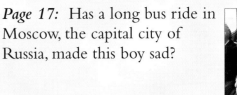

Page 17: Has a long bus ride in Moscow, the capital city of Russia, made this boy sad?

Page 12: Families join together to watch a parade in New Jersey, USA.

Page 18: Standing in a doorway in Mali, this girl smiles a shy smile.

Page 13: This girl in Hoi An, a town on the coast of Vietnam, rows a boat.

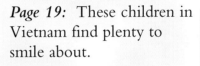

Page 19: These children in Vietnam find plenty to smile about.

Page 14: Getting up early doesn't make these Japanese preschoolers very happy.

Page 20: A boy smiles while he works in a tea shop near the Hyderabad Zoo in India.

Page 15: It's been a long trip to the market for these boys in Vilnius, Lithuania.

Page 21: Friendship brings smiles to the faces of these Canadian girls in Ontario.

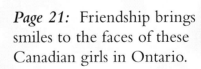

Page 16: A shy girl in South Korea hides behind some hay.

A Note to Adults on Sharing This Book

Help your child become a lifelong reader. Read this book together, taking turns as you both read out loud. Look over the photographs and choose your favourites. Sound out new words and come back to them later for review. Then try these "extensions"—activities that extend the experience of reading and build discussion and problem-solving skills.

Talk about Smiling

All around the world, you can find people smiling. This book shows smiling people in many different countries. Discuss with your child the reasons why people smile. What makes the people shown in this book smile? What people, places, or things make you and your child smile? What can you and your child do for others to make them smile?

Make a Wall of Smiles

With your child, gather pictures of people smiling. Draw pictures of people or things that make you both smile. Find pictures of smiling people in magazines. Then put all of these pictures on your wall or on a piece of poster board – to make a wall of smiles.